Stoic Time Management
Overcoming Procrastination and Mastering Focus

Table of Contents

Chapter 1. Introduction

Crave an undisturbed work-life and meaningful interaction with time? Our Special Report on "Stoic Time Management: Overcoming Procrastination and Mastering Focus," is your ticket to navigating your life's hours with wisdom and grace. Immerse yourself in strategies drawn from ancient Stoic philosophies, which have been reimagined to fit our complex, modern-day lives. This report is more than a one-time read. It's a lifelong companion, offering frameworks for effective time allocation, overcoming the hurdle of procrastination, and mastering the art of focus. Brace yourself for a transformative exploration that promises to change your perception of time, ultimately leading to a fulfilled and content life. Ready to embrace productivity like never before? Hop aboard and let's carpe diem together!

Chapter 2. Understanding Time: A Stoic Perspective

The perception of time has been a subject of intense interest throughout human history, and no less so for the ancient Stoics. In their view, one's handling of time is paramount to living a fulfilling life. Let's delve into how they approached this fascinating subject.

2.1. Time as an Elemental Commoditiy

A central tenet of Stoic philosophy is the value placed on human experiences over material possessions. This perspective extends to their regard for time. For the Stoics, time, like other resources at our disposal, is finite and should be utilized mindfully and judiciously. Every moment spent can't be retrieved - this is the reality that underpins the Stoic viewpoint.

However, while we might often lament over 'lost' time, the Stoics would remind us that time is never truly lost, rather it's invested somewhere - be it productive or otherwise. Therefore, the key is to invest our time where it matters the most: in actions that foster personal growth and collective good.

2.2. The Finite and Ethereal Quality of Time

Within the broad spectrum of this universe, human existence is brief and fleeting. Stoicism teaches us to regard the ephemeral nature of life with neither fear nor despair but with clear-eyed acknowledgment. It emphasizes the importance of accepting things as they are, including the reality that time is insubstantial and transient. Hence, to use it well is to hold mastery over it.

The Stoics use the analogy of a river to describe time. Just as one cannot touch the same waters twice in a flowing river, one cannot live the same moment twice in time's river. The realization of the finite and irretrievable quality of our time urges us to make the best of each moment.

2.3. Mindful Time Allocation

Stoic philosophers, such as Seneca, advocated for careful management of our time resources. They believed time ought to be spent on activities that contributed to purposeful living. Seneca's letters to his student Lucilius, as recorded in "On The Shortness of Life", are full of such wisdom. His counsel was to occupy one's mind with meaningful activities and steer clear from those pursuits offering empty, transient pleasure at the cost of valuable time. There are two aspects to the Stoic's approach on mindful time allocation.

Living in the Present: Stoicism stresses that the present moment is the only time over which humans have influence. The past has already happened and cannot be altered, whereas the future remains uncertain. Therefore, Stoic thought encourages individuals to live in the present, focusing their resources in optimizing the now.

Purposeful Activity: Stoics emphasize spending time on activities aligning with our life's purpose and virtue. They see virtue as the only essential good and believe that time is best utilized when employed in its service.

2.4. Futility of Procrastination

Procrastination is perceived as the postponement of efforts unto our future selves and is inherently counterintuitive from a Stoic perspective. The Stoics' emphasis on the 'present' deflates the concept of procrastination. Essentially, it's a reminder that by procrastinating, you are offloading your responsibilities onto an entity (your future self) over which you have no control.

Procrastination often stems from fear - fear of failure, discomfort, or judgment. However, Stoicism offers a weapon against this fear: acceptance and action. By accepting the inevitability of these tribulations and focusing on tangible actions, one can overcome procrastination.

2.5. Harnessing Time through Discipline and Focus

According to the Stoics, discipline is the fulcrum on which time control pivots. They advocate for a life characterized by self-control and focus, embodying the saying: "No person has the power to have everything they want, but it is in their power not to want what they don't have, and to cheerfully put to good use what they do have."

Discipline, as seen by the Stoics, is not an exercise in denial or suppression, but one in the elimination of unnecessary pursuits. It is the discerning focus on what genuinely contributes to our well-being and growth, that enables us to 'seize the day'. Practicing discipline allows us to reclaim our time, offering control over our actions rather than being at the mercy of whims and distractions.

In conclusion, the Stoic perspective of time management unfolds as a disciplined, proactive approach that prioritizes the present. It emphasizes acceptance of time's finite quality and invests it in purposeful activity, rejecting procrastination and harnessing discipline and focus. Adopting this Stoic viewpoint instills appreciation for each moment, and grants us the courage to use our time wisely, leading to a more fulfilled and content life.

Chapter 3. Rewiring Procrastination: Stoic Strategies for Action

Procrastination is the art of delaying or postponing tasks—the ones you know should be doing, or want to be doing, but find it difficult to motivate yourself to begin. It's a hurdle that universally affects individuals across different walks of life. In theory, we understand the harm it brings - a crash course in inefficiency, missed opportunities, derailed plans, and an overarching sense of guilt.

Hence, addressing procrastination is as essential as understanding its roots. Stoic philosophy offers clear, pragmatic, and time-tested advice to combat procrastination effectively. It encourages us to face the truth of our circumstances, accept our individual capability to affect them, and prioritize our actions correspondingly.

3.1. Stoic Philosophy: The Base of our Approach

Stoicism is an ancient Greek philosophy that preaches the development of self-control and fortitude as a means of overcoming destructive emotions. It doesn't teach evasion from feelings like fear or frustration. Instead, it offers guidance on how to face, analyze, and correct them emphasizing a clear, objective view of the world.

In the words of Epictetus, "We are disturbed not by things, but by the views which we take of them." Indeed, Stoicism sets the groundwork for mastering self and rewriting procrastination habits by altering our perception of them.

3.2. Understanding Procrastination: Stoic Perspective

From the Stoic viewpoint, procrastination stems from a misalignment between our rational judgment and our actions. This misalignment leads to a delay in actions, resulting in procrastination. To curb this, we can take lessons from the Stoic concepts of 'voluntary discomfort' and 'negative visualization.'

Voluntary discomfort involves the practice of intentionally placing ourselves in situations of discomfort to make us resilient and less vulnerable to change. This can include anything from cold showers, dietary changes, to abstaining from luxury.

Negative visualization, on the other hand, invites us to contemplate on the negative outcomes of not undertaking a task. This study in contrasts can fuel motivation to carry out the task promptly.

By adopting these practices, Stoicism provides a strategy to control procrastination by altering our reactions towards the tasks we often defer.

3.3. Recognizing 'The Dichotomy of Control'

The Dichotomy of Control, proposed by ancient Stoic philosopher Epictetus, is pivotal in overcoming procrastination. It helps us distinguish between things within our control (our actions, thoughts, desires) and things beyond (such as outcomes, other people's thoughts or actions).

Stoics argue that an understanding and focus on elements within our control facilitates progress and peace. Conversely, obsessing about the uncontrollable leads to discontent and procrastination. To overcome procrastination, emphasize actions within your control, and let go of the uncontrollable outcomes.

3.4. Employing 'Premeditatio Malorum': Forecasting Obstacles

Premeditatio malorum or 'premeditation of evils' is a mental exercise to anticipate potential setbacks, challenges, or adversity that might occur when performing a task. By mentally preparing ourselves for these potential obstacles, we equip ourselves to handle them more effectively—reducing the fear and the tendency to procrastinate.

Write down the challenges you anticipate and possible solutions. The act itself teaches resilience, proactiveness, and tenacity, diminishing the room for procrastination.

3.5. Practical Stoic Strategies to Overcome Procrastination

Now that we understand the Stoic philosophy and the conceptual tools it offers, let's dive into some actionable strategies.

Reframe the Task: Perception shapes our reality. By reframing a daunting task into a beneficial and meaningful one, we can motivate ourselves to start and persist.

Start Small: Break larger tasks into smaller ones. Completing these smaller tasks can build momentum and reduces the inclination to procrastinate.

Practice Voluntary Discomfort: As discussed earlier, regularly pushing yourself out of your comfort zone can increase resilience and lower the resistance to beginning or carrying out tasks.

Use Negative Visualization: Visualizing the consequences of not completing a task can be a strong motivating factor to overcome procrastination.

Acknowledge your Progress: Recognize and appreciate your efforts, however small. This acknowledgment encourages positive reinforcement and keeps the momentum going.

To conclude, harnessing the wisdom of the Stoics can prove immensely beneficial in mastering procrastination. It requires a shift in perspective, a keen understanding of control, preparation for adversities, and strategic action to overcome the hurdles. Remember, as Seneca says, "It's not that we have a short time to live, but that we waste a lot of it." Avoid procrastination and seize your time, making the most out of life.

Chapter 4. Mastering Focus: Stoics' Insight into a Disciplined Mind

'Rome wasn't built in a day,' and similarly, the practice of stoicism and mastering focus cannot be achieved in a day. Building a disciplined mind is a long and arduous journey, and we will guide you through each step of the way.

4.1. Stoicism: A Brief Overview

Before we delve into the specifics, let's shed light on the basic principles of Stoicism. Originating in Athens in the third century BC, Stoicism is a philosophy profoundly focused on inner peace, wisdom, virtue, and overall mental strength. Stoics believed in accepting life's realities and exercising total control over one's reactions, emotions, and attitudes.

4.2. The Stoic Concept of Focus

The Stoics identified focus as a crucial element of human existence. The eminent Stoic philosopher Seneca famously wrote, "It's not that we have a short time to live, but that we waste a lot of it." He argued that humans could practice and cultivate focus - a pivotal tool in time-management and living a wholesome life. This idea underlines the importance of learning to steer our attention purposefully rather than letting it diverge aimlessly.

4.3. Elements of Focus

There are three primary elements that Stoics consider crucial in developing and mastering focus.

1. Prosoche — Mindful Attention: The Stoics believed that mindful attention to the present moment, or prosoche, is the heart of focus. It refers to the consistent attentiveness to our thoughts, words, and actions, not swaying towards past regrets or future anxieties.

2. Eulabeia — Caution: This refers to cautious deliberation before making decisions or choosing paths. It involves considering the consequences and emphasizing rational thoughts over irrational impulses.

3. Synechtheia — Constancy: Stoics believed in remaining constant despite external distractions or discomforts. Setting goals and persistently working towards them help develop unwavering focus and resilience.

Now, we'll outline a series of actionable techniques based on the above principles for you to implement and master the art of focus.

4.4. Establishing Mindful Attention (Prosoche)

Mindful attention, according to Stoicism, is about nurturing the presence of mind. To cultivate Prosoche:

1. Practice Mindfulness Meditation: The practice of mindfulness meditation involves focusing your attention on your breathing and observing thoughts without judgment. It's essential to sit in a quiet place and give yourself at least ten minutes daily for this practice.

2. Engage Completely: When you perform a task, do it with complete involvement. Whether it's washing dishes, writing a report, or having a conversation, give it your full attention.

4.5. Exercising Caution (Eulabeia)

Practicing Eulabeia requires caution and a clear, thoughtful deliberation. To exercise Eulabeia:

1. Consider the Consequences: Before making a decision, think about its possible outcomes. How will it affect your present and future? This thought process will enable you to make more rational decisions and improve your focus.

2. Reflect Regularly: Take time out of your day to reflect on your actions, especially the ones that led to complications or problems. Reflection builds a cautious approach and helps avoid future blunders.

4.6. Developing Constancy (Synechtheia)

Synechtheia or constancy is about maintaining focus despite hurdles. Mindful that disruptions will occur, Stoics keep their eyes on the destination. To cultivate Synechtheia:

1. Set SMART Goals: Your goals must be Specific, Measurable, Achievable, Relevant, and Time-bound (SMART). This approach makes your objectives clear and promotes consistency.

2. Embrace Challenges: Seeing obstacles as opportunities cultivates resilience, a central tenet of Stoicism. Rather than evading difficulties, embrace them as lessons to enhance your focus and determination.

4.7. The Distractions Dilemma

In an era of smartphones and infinite internet scrolls, distractions have become a common adversary of focus. Stoics deal with this problem through the concept of 'preferred Indifference.' These are things not in our control, wherein we can express preference but should not let them disrupt our tranquility or focus. This includes managing technology wisely, setting clear boundaries, and developing healthy daily habits.

Learning to focus is a gradual process, filled with growth and epiphanies. By integrating Stoicism's timeless wisdom, we can train our minds and reclaim our focus, leading to more efficient time management and ultimately, a content life. Although the path might seem challenging, remember that as Seneca wrote, "It is not because things are difficult that we do not dare; it is because we do not dare that they are difficult." Embrace the challenge, practice these stoic insights on focus, and dare to master your mind.

Chapter 5. The Clock and You: Exploring the Relationship Between Time and Identity

From the fleeting sands of the hourglass, to the relentless ticking of the clock, time has been an inseparable companion to mankind. As we progress in our understanding of the pervasive impact time has on our lives, it becomes critical to explore the profound relationship between time and identity.

5.1. The Clock: A Socio-cultural Tool

In any society, the clock is more than a mere instrument for marking hours. It affects our perception of life, structures our daily activities, and influences our interactions within social circles. Chronemics, the study of time in communication, posits that individuals in a society inherently learn their culture's time norms and expectations.

In the western world, time is often viewed as a commodity that should be efficiently used and carefully managed. This perception reflects in phrases like "time is money", reinforcing the value placed on productivity and efficiency. Unsurprisingly, punctuality and deadline adherence are coveted traits.

Contrastingly, cyclical cultures, often found in eastern societies, perceive time as recurring sequences. Here, activities do not strictly adhere to the clock but flow with the natural rhythm of day and night. Time is viewed as ample and infinite, emphasizing relationships, contemplation, and harmony over rushed endeavors.

Understanding the socio-cultural nuances of time perception can help us navigate the course of our lives with empathy and respect for diverse worldviews.

5.2. The Metaphysics of Time

Classical philosophers from Plato to Augustine have deeply contemplated the abstract reality of time. While some philosophers argue against time's existence outside our minds, others assert its objective reality independent of our perception. Understanding these philosophical views on time can inspire you to reflect on your personal perception of time and its implications on your identity.

Is time a continuous flow or is it constituted of distinct moments? Is the future as real as the past, or is only the present moment real? Such questions, though seemingly abstract, subtly influence our attitudes towards life, human existence, and the self.

5.3. Time Consciousness and Identity

The way we perceive, measure, and allocate our time forms an integral part of our self-concept. In other words, our time consciousness significantly influences our identity.

Chronic procrastinators, for instance, likely see themselves as poor time managers who consistently struggle to meet deadlines. On the other hand, punctual individuals, often adept at task prioritization, may view themselves as productive and efficacious beings. These temporal identities not only influence our self-esteem but also affect how we behave and how others perceive us.

5.4. Biological Clocks and Natural Rhythms

Our identities are influenced by natural biological rhythms, including circadian rhythms and ultradian rhythms that govern patterns of sleep, eating and other physiological changes. Living in harmony with these natural cycles can enhance productivity and wellbeing.

Psychologically too, humans may lean towards being either "morning larks" or "night owls", and our productivity peaks may coincide with these innate preferences. Acknowledging these biological realities can lead to a more balanced life, in tune with our true selves.

5.5. Perceived Time: The Psychological Lens

Perceived time, as opposed to clock time, is how an individual experiences the passage of time. Research suggests that perception of time is subjective and varies depending upon our cognitive load, emotional state, and even the ambient temperature. The famous saying, "time flies when you're having fun" encapsulates this concept eloquently.

Being aware of these psychological influences can help in effective time management. Mindfulness techniques can aid in dilating our experience of time, potentially leading to a richer life experience.

5.6. Past, Present, Future: Shaping Identities

Our past experiences, current actions, and aspirations for the future all contribute to our identity formation. A person overly attached to past successes or failures may experience difficulty in moving forward. Conversely, focusing too much on the future can lead to anxiety or prevent us from living fully in the present moment.

A stoic approach guides us towards accepting our past, being present in the moment, and calmly anticipating the future. This can lead to a more resilient sense of self, capable of withstanding the ebbs and flows of time.

As you delve deeper into the intersection of time and identity, remember, understanding your relationship with time is a lifelong journey. Giving conscious thought to time and its influence on your self-perception can foster personal growth and bring you closer to a harmonious existence.

Time is a widespread and influential concept, its inevitability and overwhelming presence equip it with the power to shape societies and individuals alike. Exploring the relationship between time and identity, offers an expedition through philosophical terrains and psychological landscapes, marked with insights into our realization and perception of the self. Let's honor our time, for it forms the fabric of our existence.

Chapter 6. Banishing Distractions: Stoic Techniques for a Streamlined Life

Before diving into the wisdom imparted by Stoicism, it is essential to acknowledge that our reality is a veritable minefield of distractions. Our gadgets, social media accounts, commitments, fears, and even our own minds continuously vie for our attention. However, these distractions often lead to fruitless endeavors rather than aid in our growth. This chapter will provide insight into Stoic techniques, enabling you to streamline your life by cutting through the noise, focusing on what truly matters, and banishing distractions.

6.1. Embracing the Dichotomy of Control

Understanding the dichotomy of control, a key Stoic principle, can free you from many unnecessary distractions in your life. This concept asserts that some things are within our control—our actions, judgments, and reactions—while others are not—such as others' opinions, natural disasters, or death itself. Spending energy on matters that we cannot influence only fuels our stress and detracts from what we could productively exert control over.

By internalizing this principle, you can make a conscious decision to stop worrying about external factors, thus freeing up mental space. This ensures a less cluttered mind, ripe for focus and concentration.

6.2. Evoking Mindfulness: The Stoic Present

In the realm of Stoicism, mindfulness is tied to 'prosoche', which translates to attention or awareness. It's about living in the now, fixating your attention on the present moment. This easy-to-say but hard-to-master concept can effectively help in banishing distractions.

To implement this, the basic step is to consciously stay engaged in anything you're doing, keeping your thoughts from drifting away. Regular practice can train your brain to stay in the present.

6.3. Abandoning the Excess: A Life of Simplicity

To the Stoics, tranquility of mind was the product of a simple life. Having less to juggle allows your mind to concentrate on important tasks without additional cognitive load from superfluous matters.

You can institute this concept by gradually decluttering your life. Begin with your physical environment, trimming off excess possessions, and then proceed to refine your digital space, social commitments, and goals. The lesser your entanglements, the lesser will be your distractions.

6.4. Understanding Temptations: Standing Against Hedonic Adaptation

Hedonic adaptation is the human tendency to return to a set level of satisfaction after experiencing pleasure or pain. In an age of endless novelty and instant gratification, understanding and managing this concept can greatly aid in maintaining focus and reducing distractions.

Resisting the allure of novelty and cultivating the ability to find satisfaction in stability can help tackle the issue of tech distractions. Apps designed for momentary pleasure might seem pleasant initially but remember that the mind adapts; the thrill fades away and leaves you craving for more. Instead, focusing energy on less fleeting, more enriching pursuits can provide sustained satisfaction without being distracting.

6.5. Daily Contemplation: Stoic Meditation

Meditation, a common Stoic practice, focuses on reflecting upon one's principles and actions. Regular contemplation enables you to understand your distractions and discover how to reduce them.

Here, you introspect on your actions from a third person's perspective, striving for objectivity. It could be an assessment of how a particular task was handled, why a certain distraction was tough to resist, or how you can improve your response to stimuli in the future. With repeated practice, this form of meditation can help you overcome habitual distractions.

The Stoic techniques discussed here are not mere quick-fix solutions but lifelong skills that must be polished with practice. Gradually, they enable you to reclaim your mental bandwidth from unproductive distractions. In the words of the renowned Stoic philosopher, Seneca, "We should hunt out the helpful pieces of teaching and the spirited and noble-minded sayings which are capable of immediate practical application–not far far-fetched or archaic expressions or extravagant metaphors and figures of speech–and learn them so well that words become works."

Chapter 7. The Power of Now: Embracing the Stoic Art of Present Moment Awareness

Understanding the present moment is at the heart of Stoic philosophy. The Stoics believed that comprehending and living in the 'now' can be a powerful tool for managing time and life itself. Not to be confused with ignorance of the past or indifference toward the future, present moment awareness illuminates the significance of the immediate experience without being clouded by regrets of the past or worries about the future.

7.1. The Present Moment: A Stoic Perspective

In Stoicism, the concept of time is distinctively moment-centric. Renowned Stoic philosophers like Seneca and Marcus Aurelius emphasized living in accord with nature, which implies accepting the reality of the present moment. They contended that to live in the 'now' is to live in absolute reality, devoid of illusions, and unconstrained by time.

"The longest and the shortest life, then, amount to the same, for the present moment lasts the same for all and is all anyone possesses. No one can lose either the past or the future, for how can someone be deprived of what's not theirs?" - Marcus Aurelius, Meditations.

7.2. The Illusion of Time: Undoing the Knot

Our conventional perception of time tends to dwell on the past and anticipate the future, often diminishing the importance of the present moment. We define our lives by the length of our existence, our past accomplishments, and future goals. But, as the Stoics argue, time is unyielding. The past has happened, and the future is uncertain, and out of our hands; what we have true control over is the present.

Undoing the knot of this illusion of time begins when we understand that dwelling on the past contributes to regrets, while worrying about the future leads to anxiety. Both disturb our peace of mind and cloud our judgment, impeding our ability to dedicate our full focus and effort to the tasks at hand. Thus, the only way to practically manage time is by focusing on the present moment, utilizing it to the best of our abilities.

7.3. Harnessing the Power of Now: A Practical Approach

Stoicism offers practical tools and principles to help immerse ourselves in the present moment:

1. Mindfulness - Being mindful is about paying attention to the present moment, without being judgmental or allowing distractions. Mindful action ensures we are giving our best to the task at hand.

2. Dichotomy of Control - The Stoic principle of Dichotomy of Control instructs us that some things are within our control (our actions, beliefs, desires, and personal goals), and the rest are not (the past, the future, other people's actions). This makes it critical to invest our energy only in what we can control, that is, the present moment.

Implementing these principles and embodying present moment awareness leads to productive time management, eventually manifesting in quality outputs and a balanced life.

7.4. Stoic Exercises for Present Moment Awareness

Practicing Stoicism involves a range of exercises designed to cultivate mindfulness and resilience. Here are some to help maintain focus on the present:

1. Journaling: Write down your thoughts, feelings, and experiences of the day. It encourages self-reflection and mindful living.

2. Negative Visualization: Visualizing possible negative outcomes forces us to appreciate and better utilize the current moment.

3. Mindful Observation: Practice observing your surroundings without judgment as a method of stepping into the now.

7.5. Reaping the Benefits of the 'Now'

When we train ourselves to live in the present, several benefits follow. We become more focused, more productive, and more appreciative of our time. This stoic mastery of 'now' frees us from anxiety, frustration, and regret, leading to peace of mind and contentment.

Indeed, the practice of Stoicism and its emphasis on present awareness is much more than a philosophical discourse. It's a tool, a guide, and even a road map to living a fulfilled life. As we journey through the complexities of modern life, learning to leverage the power of 'now' is one of the most effective ways to navigate through our hours, days, and years. As Seneca once said, "The whole future lies in uncertainty: live immediately."

Let's ponder, apply, and live these ancient wise words, illuminating the path towards a serene and content life, tasting the bliss of every moment. Let the power of now unfold!

Chapter 8. Navigating Time: Stoic Time Management in a Digital Age

The ancient Stoics were highly adept at making the most of their time, a resource of which no one, not even the richest man, could get more. Indeed, the art of channeling time wisely is perhaps the most profound lesson we can take from Stoic philosophy. Adapting such insight to the digital age, cluttered with its numerous distractions and vast information overload, requires deliberate efforts, and it is to this end that we turn our attention.

8.1. The Principle of Dichotomy of Control

You're likely familiar with the Serenity Prayer, which implores, "Grant me the serenity to accept the things I cannot change, the courage to change the things I can, and the wisdom to know the difference." This timeless wisdom stems from the Stoic's Dichotomy of Control, a foundation of their teachings. In regards to time management, it implies we should discern between what we can and cannot control. We can control our actions, responses and thoughts, not how much time we have.

Using digital aids correctly can help us exercise control in these domains. A productivity app can help manage tasks effectively. Digital calendars can remind us of appointments, sparing us the worry of forgetting. A news aggregation tool can save us from the information deluge, giving us the news we need without wasting time on irrelevant material.

However, the Dichotomy also prompts us to accept that certain factors lie beyond our control. Internet outages, app malfunctions, or delays in others' responses may disrupt our plans. Moderating our reactions to these obstacles can keep our composure intact and our focus undeterred.

8.2. Mastering Attention in the Midst of Digital Distractions

In our digitally soaked world, where a myriad of notices vie for our attention, maintaining our focus can be a Herculean task. Especially when working on complex tasks, it helps to channel the Stoic wisdom of focusing on the present moment without being swayed by past regrets or future anxieties.

To ward off digital distractions, implement techniques like the Pomodoro Technique to work for a set time free from interruptions. Use tools that restrain intrusive notifications during these slots. After each Pomodoro session, take a short break and then resume your work.

Another Stoic technique is Negative Visualization, or envisioning the worst case scenario. When you feel the urge to check your social feed instead of working, visualize the consequences: missed deadlines, stressed relationships, job insecurities. This can deter aimless surfing and encourage focus.

8.3. Overcoming the Digital Procrastination Trap

Networking platforms, MMO games, streaming sites - the digital age is a paradise for procrastinators. When the task at hand is complex or dull, it's easy to slide into the comfort of digital distractions. However, it's helpful to remember the Stoic credo of living according to nature. For humans, flourishing hinges on constructive activities like learning, creating, bonding, nurturing, not on ceaseless scrolling or gaming.

To counter deferment, divide large tasks into manageable micro-tasks. Then, as prescribed by Stoic philosopher Seneca, "match the time to the task". Allocate specific digital slots throughout the day for internet browsing or socializing so it doesn't intrude upon productive hours.

8.4. Cultivating Virtues through Time Management

The Stoics upheld four cardinal virtues: wisdom, courage, justice, and temperance. Integrating these virtues can elevate our time management efforts.

Wisdom entails understanding the best use of time, being judicious about digital usage, and valuing productivity apps that enhance efficiency. Courage relates to our willingness to make tough choices regarding prioritizing tasks and standing against the tide of constant connectivity. Justice involves being respectful of our own and others' time. Temperance is about restrained usage of digital devices, avoiding excesses that lead to time wastage.

In summary, Stoic time management in the digital age isn't merely a set of strategies. It's a philosophy that, when internalized, can guide us to live wealthy lives where time, the ultimate currency, is well spent. The next chapters delve into how to incorporate major Stoic precepts like Memento Mori (remembering our mortality) and amor fati (love of fate) into our time management practices, providing further enlightenment on our temporal journey.

Chapter 9. Finding Balance: The Role of Stoic Philosophy in Work-Life Harmony

The pursuit of work-life balance is a modern condition, born from our complex lifestyles that often demand we play multiple roles, juggle myriad responsibilities, and press forward in an increasingly rapid, often distracting, digital age. How can ancient philosophical tenets possibly shed light on such a contemporary issue? It turns out that Stoic philosophies from thousands of years ago still hold remarkable relevance to our contemporary conundrums.

9.1. A Stoic's View on Balance

At its core, Stoicism identifies the pursuit of virtue as the sole good, with an emphasis on wisdom, courage, justice, and temperance. Stoics advocate for a tranquil life; one that is unperturbed by externalities. And it turns out, this tranquil, virtuous life is one that naturally encompasses a balance between work and the rest of life.

Stoics maintain that unnecessary wants and desires make us lose focus from what's really important: our inner self, our reactions and our virtues. This includes learning when to work, when to pause, when to immerse ourselves in family or solitude, and when to push further or pull back.

9.2. Understanding Externals

One core tenet of Stoicism is understanding the difference between things within our control—our actions, beliefs, desires, and personal efforts—and things outside of our control—other people's actions, events governed by nature, and the past. Anything external to the mind, Stoics argue, is indifferent and should not disturb our inner peace.

In applying this to work-life balance, we learn to accept that we can't control everything in our work environment. Market fluctuations, corporate restructuring, demanding bosses, or difficult colleagues—these aren't things we can significantly, if at all, control.

Stoic philosophy teaches us to invest energy and time in areas where we can make a difference, which practically equates to focusing on performing our tasks effectively and with integrity, while striving to become better at what we do. This shift in focus from uncontrollable externals to personal performance can alleviate work-related stress and enhance satisfaction with professional life.

9.3. Embracing Impermanence

Another significant Stoic cornerstone is embracing the concept of impermanence, a perspective that can greatly contribute to a sense of work-life balance. Stoicism teaches us to understand and accept that change is the only constant. In the context of a career, this could mean periods of excessive workloads, phases of relative calm, or even full transformation within the role or job itself. Recognizing the transient nature of these situations can help manage stress and encourage us to patiently persevere, knowing that no circumstance, whether favorable or not, is permanent.

9.4. Choosing Our Response

Epictetus famously asserted, "It's not what happens to you, but how you react to it that matters." Stoicism empowers individuals to choose their responses to situations, thereby implying that our mood or state of mind is not a direct result of our circumstances but rather how we interpret and react to them.

In the context of work-life balance, this means shifting the focus from trying to control external conditions to managing our reactions to them. If work becomes stressful, Stoics remind us that we can choose to respond with patience and resilience, as opposed to panic or frustration.

9.5. Embracing Digital Minimalism

In today's age of digital distractions, ancient Stoicism also has a surprisingly modern application: digital minimalism. Stoics were minimalists who believed in focusing on necessities and urged to avoid unnecessary desires and distractions. In a time of constant emails, continuous social media updates, and digital noise, embracing Stoic principles can mean cultivating a focused approach to digital tools and communications. This minimalistic approach can significantly reduce digital distractions and further bolster work-life balance.

9.6. Stoic Exercises for Work-Life Balance

Finally, practicing Stoic exercises can equip us in our pursuit for work-life balance. One such practice is Stoic meditation, which involves reflecting on our day, understanding what went well and what didn't, and preparing ourselves for similar situations we might encounter in the future.

Another exercise is voluntary discomfort. By periodically embracing discomfort, we build resilience to the stresses at work, thereby reducing the risk of burnout. Whether it's taking the stairs instead of the elevator or foregoing a convenient service for a more time-consuming manual one, these small exercises strengthen our ability to handle bigger challenges at work.

In conclusion, finding a work-life balance isn't about rigid structures or strict boundaries, but about developing an effective mindset that can adapt to changing roles and environments. It's about knowing what to care about, how to react to change, and how to protect ourselves from unnecessary stressors. Stoic philosophy holds invaluable wisdom that can guide us through the labyrinth of work-life balance. Its insights extend far beyond the typical dichotomy of work or life, revealing how we, both as workers and beings striving for contentment, can achieve tranquility and satisfaction in all dimensions of life.

Chapter 10. Resilience in the Face of Setbacks: Stoic Approaches to Persisting Through Obstacles

In the smooth march of life, the inevitability of bumps and obstacles is a given. They appear in various shapes and forms - project setbacks, personal issues, unexpected life events. It is worth noting that these trials and tribulations are not inherently undesirable; instead, they test and develop our resilience. The ancient Stoics recognized this axiom, offering timeless wisdom to help us navigate through such obstacles with constructive responses, rather than reactive flinches.

In an exploration of these Stoic principles, we will dive into the following three sub-topics, each providing integral insights:

10.1. Building a Steadfast Mindset

The first pillar to resilience is cultivating a formidable mindset - one that sees obstacles as opportunities and setbacks as spaces for growth. Epictetus, a Stoic philosopher, famously stated, "It's not what happens to you, but how you react to it that matters."

Our mind is the ultimate battlement that either succumbs to or withstands the onslaught of challenges. The Stoics emphasized nurturing an indifference towards circumstances beyond our control while focusing on our responses and actions. They opined that setbacks do not diminish us; rather, our attitude toward them defines our resilience.

Consider the mindset as a personal garden. We must endeavor to eliminate weeds (negative thoughts) and plant seeds of positivity and perseverance. It is an ongoing process of tending to our mental state, ensuring it remains steadfast in the face of adversity. Cultivating such a mindset requires consistent introspection, practice, and reconditioning our thought processes.

10.2. Embracing Change and Uncertainty

Change is the sole constant in the universe — a basic tenet of Stoic philosophy. If we anticipate and accept this, we can better prepare ourselves to recover from setbacks. Resisting change or hankering after permanency only brews distress. Instead, the Stoics advised embracing change with acceptance and adaptability.

Marcus Aurelius, a Roman emperor and Stoic philosopher, said, "The universe is change; our life is what our thoughts make it.". Contemplate on this, and embrace the flux of life, allowing it to shape, not shatter, our resilience.

While it is reasonable to speculate on potential outcomes, excessive worry for the future robs us of our present. Stoicism aligns with the concept of being 'present-minded,' focusing on tasks at hand rather than brooding over uncertainties. This dedication to the present moment helps stave off stress and anxiety bred from forecasting future troubles, fostering strength in the face of setbacks.

10.3. Actionable Steps for Resilience

Now that we have discussed the essential precepts to foster a resilient mindset let's lay down some practical steps derived from Stoicism:

1. Foster Indifference Towards External Circumstances: Often, we let our external environment dictate our internal state. Stoics

advise against this. Strive to remain equanimity and composed, no matter the circumstance.

2. Maintain Inner Dialogue: Consistently evaluate your thought process. Recognize if an emotion is a natural response or an exaggerated reaction to a situation, and adjust your thoughts accordingly.

3. Practice Discomfort: Epictetus suggested occasional voluntary discomfort to prepare for unforeseen hardships. This could be as simple as skipping a meal or two, taking a cold shower, or sleeping on a hard floor. This practice aids in strengthening mental fortitude.

4. Reflect and Learn: Every setback is a potential teacher. Rather than resisting them, reflect on the lessons they offer and harness them for future betterment.

Combining these Stoic principles with strategic and tactical practices can equip you with resilience mechanisms that can help you weather setbacks with grace and fortitude.

To sum up, Stoic teachings on resilience in the face of setbacks advocate for a shift in perspective, embracing change, and developing an actionable resilience plan. Adherence to these can coordinate your life compass towards a more steadfast destination. While setbacks may seem daunting, remember the wisdom of the Stoic philosopher Seneca who said, "A gem cannot be polished without friction, nor a man perfected without trials." Steer through life with resilience, and witness each setback morph into a stepping stone to ultimately shape your best self.

Chapter 11. Journey to Self-Mastery: Stoicism for Personal Growth and Productivity

In the realm of ancient guidelines, Stoicism is viewed as a robust framework for personal growth and productivity. Born in the chaos of a bygone era, these principles are timeless, providing valuable coping mechanisms in the face of modern life's complexities.

11.1. Embracing the Stoic Philosophy

Stoicism is a philosophical school of thought that originated in Athens, Greece, around 3rd Century BCE. Its teachings hold relevance even today due to its universal applicability. This philosophy's core lies in focusing on what you can control—your actions and thoughts—and abstaining from fretting over things beyond your control. This acceptance results in less stress and anxiety, boosting mental stability, which inevitably leads to a surge in productivity levels.

While understanding Stoicism, it's fundamental to recognize its four cardinal virtues: wisdom, courage, justice, and temperance. Applying these virtues to time management can transform the way you perceive and interact with time in your personal and professional life.

11.2. Stoicism and Time Management

Time, arguably our most valuable resource, needs mindful handling. Stoicism fosters this attentiveness and aids individuals in grasping its essence. There lies a two-pronged issue in the management of time: the short supply of time and our overwhelming demands on it.

The practice of Stoicism helps us assess the paradoxical nature of time better. It encourages eliminating the superfluous from life, thereby freeing up more time for tasks that truly matter. However, it doesn't promote relentless striving towards productivity but rather an attempt to strike a balance between our personal and professional lives.

The integration of Stoic principles into time management strategies involves two primary aspects: overcoming procrastination and mastering the art of focus.

11.3. Overcoming Procrastination

A central theme in Stoicism is 'Memento Mori,' which translates to 'Remember you must die.' This macabre reminder is not to breed fear but rather to highlight the fleeting nature of time. The inevitability of death serves as a reminder that procrastination is a gross disservice to our limited time, keeping us from accomplishments and personal growth.

Procrastination is not solely a failure of time management but also a failure in managing emotions. Stoicism helps confront avoidance, teaching us to face our responsibilities head-on.

Listed below are some Stoic techniques to combat procrastination:

- 'Premeditatio Malorum', or the premeditation of evils: Visualize the outcome of inaction and then contrast this with the rewards of action. This exercise brings clarity and encourages immediate movement toward the task.

- 'Voluntary Discomfort': Embrace minor discomfort to reduce the fear of adversity. This training makes tasks seem less daunting, mitigating procrastination.

- 'Dichotomy of Control': Discerning between what we can control and what we cannot helps in setting clear, manageable goals, thus minimizing procrastination.

11.4. Mastering the Art of Focus

The ability to anchor our attention is critical for productivity. It is easy to scatter our focus among a myriad of distractions that vie for our time. Stoicism underscores the importance of 'present moment focus,' helping curtail the inflow of distracting thoughts.

The Stoic practice of mindfulness, 'Prosoche,' focuses on present actions and thoughts, devoid of judgments and distractions. Sharp focus on the task at hand leads to enhanced productivity and timely completion of tasks. This process allows for mindful allocation of time and helps foster a sense of fulfillment.

The following Stoic practices can be leveraged to aid focus:

- 'Negative Visualization': Imagine the worst possible outcome. This contemplative state keeps the mind focused, realizing the importance of the task and the potential fallout of a lack of attention.

- 'Mindfulness (Prosoche)': Practice mindfulness, which accentuates the experience of the present moment, enhancing immersion in the current task.

- 'Voluntary Hardship': Intentionally seek experiences that are difficult. This deliberate challenge strengthens mental resilience and enhances focus.

In summary, Stoicism applies ancient wisdom to contemporary nuances, setting the foundation for a healthier approach to time management and personal productivity. Through practices such as overcoming procrastination and mastering focus, every individual can wield the tool that is time more effectively, leading to personal growth and a more fulfilled life. Remembering that today is a non-renewable resource, let's seize it. For, as Seneca the Stoic philosopher once said, "It's not that we have a short time to live, but that we waste a lot of it."

www.ingramcontent.com/pod-product-compliance
Lightning Source LLC
Chambersburg PA
CBHW072222290526
45794CB00007B/2857